HOLYWELL
and District

A Portrait in Old Picture Postcards

by

David Wilkes

S.B. Publications
1992

First published in 1992 by S.B. Publications
Unit 2, The Old Station Yard, Pipe Gate, Market Drayton, Shropshire TF9 4HY

ISBN: 1 85770 024 4

Typeset and printed in Great Britain by Stowes the Printers, Longton, Stoke-on-Trent, Staffordshire ST3 1HB

CONTENTS

CONTENTS: continued

Page

CONTENTS: continued

ACKNOWLEDGEMENTS

The author is indebted to the following, without whose help and support this book would not have been possible:

Nigel Acott, Dr Ken Davies, Amy England, Astley Jones, Hilda Jones, Josephine Jones, Maris Jones, Ed Newall, Derek Richardson, Edwina Sale, Owen Wilkes, Ann & Keith Williams, and Mr J L Williams.

County Records Office, Hawarden

Dr Harry Bernard-Smith for editorial work

Special thanks to my wife Adele and my daughters, Lisa, Stephanie, Samantha, and Eluned for their continuing support, and to all the residents of Holywell and District who contributed in any way to this publication.

INTRODUCTION

In compiling this volume of Holywell and District in old postcards and photographs, I have tried to pass on some of the pleasure I have gained over the past twenty years in collecting and researching postcards, photographs, and other mementoes of the area. I hope, too, that the pictures and information contained within these pages will rekindle a memory or two for those people who will recall from their childhood many of the scenes and events illustrated.

The book takes us on a short trip around the locality, stopping momentarily to look at day-to-day life, industry, and commerce in the various towns and villages in a period spanning the reigns of six monarchs. The remainder of this introduction is taken from Pigot's *North Wales Directory (1835)*, which gives a brief insight into how Victorian commentators would have seen the area.

'Holywell is a thriving market-town, in the parish of its name, in the county of Flint; 207 miles NW from London, 70 E from Holyhead, 19 NW from Chester, 5 NW from Flint, and the like distance NE from Caerwys; eligibly situate for the purposes of trade, about two miles from the banks of the Dee, and about three and a half from Bagillt Ferry. In the early part of the eighteenth century, this place is described by Walker as a poor-looking village, its streets unpaved, the houses thatched with straw, and enjoying no market. The present town exhibits a most gratifying contrast — it has the best market in this part of North Wales, the houses are neat and well built, and those forming its main street, which is of considerable length, running from east to west, are for the most part lighted with gas. From an early date, Holywell has been celebrated for its fine spring of water, called 'St Winifred's Well', of which many a wonderful tale is related; but whatever tradition says of it, it is certainly a very remarkable and interesting spring, bursting forth with great rapidity from under a hill, and is said to discharge upwards of twenty tons of water a minute; it rises in a basin twelve feet by seven, over which is raised a chapel, supported by light Gothic pillars, built by the Countess of Derby, mother of Henry VII. The roof over the well is finely carved in stone, with the legend of St Winifred, embellished with seven pieces of sculpture, relating to the Stanley family; it is also hung round with crutches, said to have been left by persons who were cured by resorting to this spring. Although the waters have long since lost their reputation for miraculous healing powers, they are now much and deservedly esteemed by the manufacturer; for the stream, in its short course to the river Dee, supplies and turns many mills for cotton works, forges, etc. The trade of the town consists chiefly in the manufacture of cotton goods, the smelting of lead, rolling of copper, and making of paper; here are also several iron and brass

INTRODUCTION: continued

foundries; and lead, calamine, limestone, and coal are found in the immediate neighbourhood; which latter gives additional value to all the rest. Holywell shares with Flint and other places (named in the description of the latter town), in the privilege of returning one member to parliament.

'The places of worship are the parish church, three chapels for dissenters, and one for Roman Catholics; the church, which is dedicated to St Winifred, and situate on the hill over the well, is a neat edifice; the living is a vicarage, in the patronage of the principal and fellows of Jesus College, Oxford, and incumbency of the Rev. John Jones. A free grammar school, one conducted upon the national plan, and a dispensary, are the principal charities. Near the town is Mostyn Hall, the seat of the Hon. E M L Mostyn, MP, built prior to the reign of Henry VI, not more worthy of notice from its antiquity than the singularity of its architecture: this house is also remarkable as the place where Henry, Earl of Richmond, afterwards Henry VII, laid the foundation of his plan to overthrow the house of York, which he afterwards carried into effect.

'About a mile east from Holywell are the remains of Basingwerk Abbey (frequently called Greenfield monastery), beautifully situate on a gentle eminence commanding a fine view of the surrounding country and the Chester canal. In the reigns of Henry II and Edward I this abbey was one of great note, as the abbots held their regular parliaments here, and also discharged other public duties. The market, which is held on Friday, is exceedingly well attended; the fairs are not so well supported — they take place on the 23rd March, Trinity Tuesday, and the 21st of September. The parish and town of Holywell contained, in 1821, 8,309 inhabitants, and in 1831, 8,969.

'Bagillt, in the parish of Holywell, from which town it is distant three miles and a half, is a long and straggling village, running parallel with the river Dee, over which is a ferry to Parkgate. Here are extensive smelting works and coal mines, which give employment to many of the inhabitants. the methodists, calvinists, and independents have each a place of worship. The population returns are made up with those of Holywell parish — the number of inhabitants in the village amount to about 1,200.'

HIGH STREET, HOLYWELL, 1910

The building on the extreme right, No 42, was once a public house, the Britannia Inn. In 1904 its licence was withdrawn, and it became a chemist's shop. In 1907, however, a Rhyl dentist advertised his services in the premises, announcing 'teeth extracted painlessly with the latest anaesthetics, nitrous oxide and oxygen gas, ethyl-chloride, etc.' Other prominent buildings in this part of High Street are Lambert's Hotel (next to the bank) and, at the head of the street, the Hotel Victoria, formerly the King's Arms. The replacement of the cobbled pavements by concrete slabs, begun in July 1909, was clearly not yet complete.

1

HIGH STREET, HOLYWELL, c.1911

The replacement of the cobbles was all but finished, and more notice of the photographer was taken on this occasion. Evan Williams the barber has left his chair and stands in his white apron outside his shop in the right foreground. The large carved wooden lion over the portico of the Red Lion inn to the left of the picture caused a minor sensation in April 1912. In an article headlined 'The collapse of the Lion', the *Observer* described how the carving had fallen suddenly on to the pavement and smashed, reporting: 'For very many years the wooden figure had been a distinguished feature of the Hotel. It was looked upon as one of the historic figures of Old Holywell.'

High Street from Station
Holywell No 13508

HIGH STREET, HOLYWELL, c.1920

This view, looking towards Cross Street, shows how rapidly the motor car was replacing the horse and cart. To the right stand the entrance and portico of the Midland Bank, while at the extreme left a break in the roof line marks the place where the town's cycle depot and Tom Edge's gents' hairdresser's shop stood until they were destroyed by fire in 1912. Holywell Fire Brigade attended the blaze, but found no water available for their pumps. The Flint brigade were summoned but could not turn out because they had no horses. Mold Fire Brigade were more successful, setting out after acquiring five horses from a local livery stable, but they did not arrive until two and a half hours after the fire started. Only the efforts of the townspeople prevented the conflagration from spreading.

PRINCE OF WALES THEATRE

Replacing the Empire Electric Picture Palace as the town's principal cinema, the Prince of Wales Theatre and Cinema opened in Station Road at the rear of the Boar's Head in January 1922. It was described as having the latest in comfort, heating, and ventilation. Films were shown by back projection, which was said 'to do away with eye strain'. By 1939 the prices of seats had risen to 6d, 9d, 1/-, and 1/3. The September 1955 programme included Arthur Askey and Thora Hird in *The Love Match*, John Mills and Eric Portman in *The Colditz Story*, and Johnny Weissmuller in *Tarzan and His Mate*. After a spell as a supermarket, the theatre was finally destroyed by fire.

PEN-Y-BALL HILL, HOLYWELL.

PEN Y BALL HILL, c.1925

Viewed here from the Strand during the mid-1920s, the Prince of Wales Theatre (centre) dwarfs the scene. In the foreground stands the 'tower lift'; this was used to raise heavy luggage and parcels to the top of the adjacent bridge spanning the station and on to Station Road for local delivery. To the left of the picture can be seen Bank Place. Many of the cottages here were recently demolished to make way for the Holywell inner ring road. Pen y Ball Hill rises to the horizon behind the theatre.

WELL STREET, 1908

One of many postcards produced by the Scotcher family, this view was taken from Cross Street; Well Street stretches off to the right, while the road on the left led to Chapel Street. On the left the tall building with the porch was the Antelope Inn, outside which once stood a Round House or lock-up, where drunks were held overnight awaiting trial and which was clearly marked on John Wood's 1833 map of Holywell. The Antelope closed in 1909 and, with many other nearby buildings, has been demolished. The inner ring road now divides the present Well Street.

CASTLE HILL

Castle Hill in Lower Well Street derives its name from the castle built by Ranulf III, Earl of Chester, in 1209 to protect the Well during the wars with the Welsh princes. In the 1730s Holywell's first workhouse was established on the hill, while John Wood's 1833 map highlights there a number of buildings belonging to the Marquis of Westminster. This early 1920s postcard shows in the centre the entrance to Castle Hill, now the site of the parish church hall and the curate's house.

RED HOUSES

Holywell has lost many of the terraced cottages, hidden squares, and yards in which small communities flourished during the 18th, 19th, and early 20th centuries. Swan Court, Blue Bell Yard, Caernarfon Castle Yard, Bank Place, Allen Square, Rose Hill, Boar's Head Yard, and Brynford Terrace have all gone. So, too, have Red Houses on the Old Chester Road. The two-storey dwellings shown here are Nos 1 to 4, while Nos 5 to 8 behind them have three storeys. Some of the larger houses had cellars.

RED HOUSES

Another view of Red Houses, this time from the rear of Nos 1 to 4, pictured here on the right. In the centre can be seen the front view of Nos 15 and 16. The downspouts came only three quarters of the way down the wall; this was to enable a water barrel to be placed under the spout to collect rainwater. Piped water did not come to Holywell until the 1920s, although many houses remained without it until well into the 1950s, residents having to fetch their supplies from local standpipes.

CHAPEL STREET

Situated between New Road (Well Hill) and Well Street, Chapel Street was almost a community in itself. The houses seen here in 1957 comprised two rooms upstairs, two downstairs, and a coal cellar. The archway and alley pictured midway down the row led to a yard at the rear of the street, containing the outside 'dry toilets' and the clothes lines.

A BIT OF OLD HOLYWELL, c.1905

The ruins of the old windmill at Pen y Maes have for many years been a local landmark. Before its closure in the 1890s, townspeople took their corn there to be ground into flour, for which service the miller would take one tenth of the grain as payment. This postcard shows the mill without its roof or sails. Despite the ravages of time and threats of demolition, the windmill survives today, the main structure having been restored and re-roofed by its present owner, Keith Edgeley.

A bit of Old Ho...

Procession to Proclamation of King George V at Holywell. May 11th 1910   Scatcher's Series

PROCLAMATION OF KING GEORGE V, 1910

On 11 May 1910, following the death of his father King Edward VII, the official reading in Holywell of the Proclamation of King George V took place in front of the Town Hall. The proceedings began with a procession down High Street from Victoria Square. Pictured leading the procession are Thomas Waterhouse, JP, Chairman of Holywell Urban District Council, T Roberts, Vice-Chairman, and Kerfoot Roberts, Clerk; they are followed by other councillors and county magistrates.

Proclamation of King George V at Holywell. May 11th 1910.   Scotcher's Series.

PROCLAMATION OF KING GEORGE V, 1910

Outside the Town Hall had been erected a temporary stage covered in purple cloth, a large crowd had gathered, and the Territorials, Scouts, and Boys' Brigade formed a square. Once the dignitaries had taken their positions a bugler sounded the 'Alert', and the Chairman, Thomas Waterhouse, JP, read the Proclamation of King George V's accession. The crowd sang 'God Save the King' and gave a rousing cheer for Queen Mary. Then the town's flags, which had been run to the masthead during the proclamation, were returned to half-mast in continued mourning for the death of the late King Edward VII.

Funeral Procession of King Edward VII. Holywell. May 20th 1910.   Scotcher's Series

FUNERAL PROCESSION, 1910

King Edward VII was buried on 20 May 1910, and memorial processions and services were held throughout the country. In Holywell all businesses were closed and licensed houses remained shut from 10.00am to 6.00pm. At 12.30pm a procession representing townsfolk and many local organisations formed in High Street before going to the parish church. The Independent Order of Oddfellows (Lord Mostyn Lodge) wore sprigs of thyme in their buttonholes and black sashes; the Ancient Order of St David wore black sashes and hatbands; the Order of Buffaloes had ivy leaves with the initials of the Order in silver. Above, a section of the parade makes its way towards Well Street.

HOLYWELL EISTEDDFOD, 1909

On August Bank Holiday 1909, on land belonging to a Mrs Owens of Strand Farm, the town held an eisteddfod in aid of the Welsh Congregational Church. One of the day's highlights was a Brass Band March contest in High Street, first prize going to the Welsh Flannel Mills Silver Band. Other competitions included instrumental and vocal solos, choirs, recitations, essays, and craftwork. Prizes ranged from cash to medals, silver cups, and conductors' batons. Connah's Quay Silver Prize Band won £8 and a gold medal for their conductor for gaining first place in the Brass Band competition, while Gronant Juvenile School took the £4 award for best Juvenile Choir. The £10 cheque pictured here was won by the Prescot and District Choral Society, whose conductor, Mr J D Williams, gained the silver cup.

ROMAN CATHOLIC PROCESSION, 1914

During the annual celebration of her Feast day, a procession winds its way down Well Hill towards St Winefride's Well. Roman Catholics travelled from all parts of the country to take part, often forming national groups. On 19 August 1897, the *Flintshire Observer* reported: 'One of the most picturesque pilgrimages that has visited Holywell this season was made on Monday last by the Italian Colony from Goulders Street Church, Manchester.' The women wore national costume and head dress of gaily-embroidered shawls, with three girls wearing crowns. On reaching Holywell station, the Italian pilgrimage walked in procession to the Well, carrying banners, and escorting a large statue decorated with flowers.

ROMAN CATHOLIC PROCESSION, 1914

Many postcards were produced of pilgrimages and processions to St Winefride's Well, and this one depicts a different section from that shown on the preceding page. It was usual to publish these scenes in sets of six, to be sold to the public for a few pence a set. Many of the buildings shown here have long disappeared; typical were St Winefride's Terrace, and Greenfield Row in what was then known as Greenfield Street. Several public houses lined the route to the Well, offering their hospitality to visitors. Most notable were the Talacre Arms, the Harp Inn, and the Rock Inn, although of these only the first survives today.

VISIT OF THE PRINCE OF UGANDA, 1914

During the summer of 1914, Holywell welcomed a party of distinguished visitors who were touring Britain. They included Prince Joseph, Prince of Uganda, his father-in-law and Regent, Prince Stanislaus Mirgwana, Chief Alexis Pokino, and Bishop Hanlon. During their two-day stay the party lived at Lambert's Hotel and visited the convent and monastery at Pantasaph, St Winefride's Well, and the Welsh Flannel Mills. Pictured here at the Well. Prince Joseph and Bishop Hanlon are in the centre, with Prince Stanislaus and Chief Alexis to their left. Other dignitaries were Messrs T and M Waterhouse, Father Ryan, and the Reverend Dr Hook.

TALACRE ARMS, c.1890

Situated almost halfway down Well Hill, the inn first appears in *Worrall's Trade Directory* of 1874, when the licensee was named as Wm Jones. In 1904 it was owned by Sir Pyers Mostyn as a house tied to St Winefride's Brewery Co., Holywell. In 1928 an auction document described the Talacre Arms as follows. 'The net annual income is £16.10s.0d. The accommodation includes: Ground floor — bar, tap room, smoke room, cellar, and scullery; First floor — landings, sitting room, and two bedrooms; Second floor — landings, four bedrooms, and box room; Outside yard with double gates, open lean-to shed, brick built stables, urinal, two privies, and adjoining cottage. The adjacent terraced row is Castle View, built in 1861.

WELL HOUSE, c.1915

Well House was for many years the gateway of St Winefride's Well, regarded as the Welsh Lourdes. Every year ailing pilgrims would queue outside, waiting to bathe in the healing waters in the hope of finding a remedy. The walls of the shrine were once lined with crutches discarded by those who believed themselves cured. In 1896 a letter from a nurse at the Ormskirk Workhouse Infirmary referred to an inmate alleged to have been healed by bathing in the well on Good Friday. 'Pritchard was a sufferer for years with a dilated stomach....and the Doctor pronounced his case hopeless and incurable. When he stepped into the Well he felt a thrill of joy....and he was cured.'

CORONATION DAY 1953

The children of West Drive and Pen y Ball Street celebrated with a party in the school room of Bethel Chapel, each child receiving a commemorative medal. This photograph of the children and organisers was taken outside the main entrance. With the help of the Clerk to Holywell Town Council, Astley Jones (far left, back row), we have discovered some of their names: Astley Jones, Roger Blackwell, Gary Blackwell, Peter Davies, May Thomas, Arfon Davies, Violet Williams, Pat Graham (Davies), Mona Griffiths, Norman Williams, Gwennie Jones, Peter Staley, Blodwen Davies, Mrs Staley, Mrs Sealeaf, Wyn Edwards, Jane Davies, Ann Thomas, Kathleen Tune, Margaret Davies, Sandra Davies, Ken Davies, Lawrence Tune, David Williams, Alan Stokes, Keith Edwards, Robert Davies, Kevin Wilson, Graham Blackwell, Mike Davies, Alvar Griffiths, Bryn Jones, Tom Tune, Billy Wright, and Colin Edwards.

21

THIS WILL BE HANDY, I FEEL QUITE SURE, FOR THE MORNING AFTER THE THE NIGHT BEFORE.

AT HOLYWELL.

THE NIGHT BEFORE, 1919

The sending home of humorous or comic postcards to friends has long been a favourite pastime with holidaymakers. Postcard collecting had become a major hobby throughout the Edwardian period and the First World War, and Holywell traders, like those throughout the rest of the country, sold many hundreds of different cards depicting various themes, scenes, and topical trends. This card was appropriate at the time, for Holywell was noted for the abundance of its public houses, and it is likely that the town did as brisk a trade in Seidlitz powders as it did in postcards. The powders, a laxative aperient of two medicines mixed separately with water and then poured together to effervesce, were supposedly helpful in curing hangovers.

'GIMME 'OSSES', 1912

Locally, this postcard was especially topical, for certain prominent Holywell figures were forecasting the end of the horse. In May 1911 the proprietor of the Kings Head Hotel, Captain Frank Salter, who also ran the local horse-drawn bus service, addressed a public meeting, declaring that the proposed introduction of a service of motor vehicles would be a disaster for the town. He claimed that grocers, blacksmiths, saddlers, and carriage makers and painters would lose much of their business. The meeting decided that char-a-bancs were not as reliable as the horse, and a petition was presented to the licensing committee of the Urban District Council — who chose to grant the application.

EASTER PEACE, 1919

As part of the peace and victory celebrations at the end of the Great War, the Parish Church gave this card to the parishioners of Holywell and Greenfield. Special services were held throughout Easter at the Parish Church, St Peter's, and Holy Trinity, Greenfield, and by the other denominations in the district. The main festivities took place on 19 July, however, when a parade in High Street was followed by celebrations on the Ffordd Fer sports field. The more unusual events included 'blind boxing' and 'tilting the bucket'. In the evening, after having been accused of atrocities against humanity and suitably tried in front of the Town Hall, an effigy of the ex-Kaiser was taken by carriage to the field and burnt.

EASTER COMMUNION, 1920

For Easter 1920 the Parish Church commissioned a second postcard. This example, like that of 1919, bears on the reverse the name 'Hughes — Builder' and the address '36 Whitford Street'. Not only was Easter one of the most important dates in the church calendar; it also meant the arrival of a circus or fair, usually on Howard's Field, Halkyn Street. 1911 saw the visit of Bostock and Wombwell's Travelling Zoo, boasting 'the finest and largest lions of all ages in Europe today'. The zoo also had tigers, leopards, bears, hyenas, wolves, jaguars, a waggon-load of monkeys, and foreign birds. There were elephants and camels for children to ride on, and three lion tamers gave regular performances

'JOHNNY BARA', 1935

Once well-known in the Holywell area, John Williams was known locally as 'Johnny Bara' — Johnny Bread. His first bakery was opposite St Winefride's Well. He later moved a few yards down the road to Clifton Bakery, and his delivery round covered much of the district. Pictured here with his Morris van outside Holywell Textile Mills, Johnny was a favourite with the children, always managing to find a broken cake or two for them. A speciality, 'Fat Neddies', was greatly enjoyed by families; squares of cake an inch thick and made from off-cuts of dough and currants, they cost a penny each. By the 1950s his van was a familiar sight on many new housing estates such as the Holway. John Williams died in 1963 after more than half a century in the business.

THE ALEXANDRA INN, c.1900

Sited in Bryncelyn, almost midway between Holywell and Greenfield, the inn was owned by St Winefride's Brewery Company. This photograph shows above the door the name of John Ames as licensee, and he is possibly the bearded gentleman in the foreground. *Worrall's Trade Directory* of 1874 lists him as already being landlord then. Downstairs, the Alexandra possessed a bar, smoke room, two snugs, a ground-floor cellar, kitchen, and washhouse; upstairs were a clubroom — used as a meeting-place by the local lodge of the Loyal Order of Ancient Shepherds — and three bedrooms. The outside yard contained a urinal, privy, and garden.

Holywell from the Air, Showing St. Winefred's Ch. Parish Church & Greenfield Rd.

91084

HOLYWELL FROM THE AIR

This aerial postcard shows sections of the town mentioned in previous pages. The large concentration of buildings in the centre is straddled by Well Street and New Road (Well Hill). Chapel Street, Whitford Street, and the Parish Church can also be seen. The hexagonal Bryn Zion Chapel, said to have seating for 400 people, is recognisable to the left of the picture. In the top right-hand corner are Battery Row and Crescent Mill, with the Holywell branch line winding its way up the Greenfield Valley. The bottom left-hand corner shows Pen y Ball Street leading to Pen y Ball Hill.

HIGH STREET FROM THE AIR

This view includes many buildings characteristic of old Holywell. Prominent are the recently-opened Prince of Wales Theatre and Cinema, the Midland Bank (formerly the White Horse Hotel), Bank Place, the observation tower in Tower Gardens, and Rehobeth Chapel in Whitford Street. Many of the shop frontages on the north side of High Street are quite clear, from Parry and Morris' ironmongers at No 1 to Sefton's the chemist. On the south side (centre) is the Town Hall, with the Market Hall and Blue Bell Yard to the rear.

HOLYWELL FROM PEN Y BALL

The panorama of Holywell and Greenfield during the 1950s illustrates the ever-changing face of the area. The chimneys and buildings of the Courtaulds plant at Greenfield no longer dominate the coastline as they do in this picture, and many of the terraced cottages have been replaced by housing estates such as the Strand, shown here overlooking the Greenfield Valley.

CARDING DEPARTMENT, c. 1890

The textile industry played a major part in Holywell's economy for more than two centuries, employing hundreds of workers. One of the early stages of production is 'carding', where the wool passes through a machine with revolving cylinders to be teased out into a fine web of intermingled fibres before it is spun. This rare scene shows the carding machines at work.

CRESCENT MILL, c.1890

The factory, a six-storey cotton mill, was built in 1790, the fourth to be erected in the Greenfield Valley, and by 1832 it was producing thirty per cent of the spun cotton in the Valley. Power for the machinery was provided by a waterwheel, 15ft high and 10ft wide. Some of the workers are here pictured in the weaving shed, where one of the drawbacks was the enormous amount of noise created by the looms and other machinery. In many mills, lip-reading was the only way of conducting a conversation. Crescent Mill eventually became derelict, and was demolished in the late 1950s.

5311. Gwalia Hosiery Mill, Holywell. ...cher's Series.

THE GWALIA HOSIERY COMPANY

Formed in 1897, the company was concerned with the machine knitting of woollen underclothing of every description. By 1900 it employed fifty people at the Crescent Mill, and between March and May of that year 16,000 shirts were ordered for troops fighting in the Boer War. This early photograph shows the main sewing room at the mill. Its two rows of foot-operated sewing machines were worked by skilled women and girls. The company eventually moved to the Battery Mills site further down the Greenfield Valley. There they continued producing shirts and the like until the mid-1950s, when a fire put them out of business.

33

THE GWALIA HOSIERY COMPANY, 1947

Management & Staff, left to right: *Back row*: Pat Ward, Nancy Jones, Thelma Bailey, Eunice Evans, Evelyn Hibbert, Olwen Youd, Sheila Vickers, Sylvia Daniels, Susan Davies. *Middle row*: Margaret Barrett, Frances Butler, Brenda Dodd, Audrey Jones, Arthur Blythin, Mair Foulkes, Hazel Renshaw, Myfanwy Roberts, Marjorie Lloyd, June Lloyd, Gwyneth Morgan, Enid Jones. *Front row*: Mair Lloyd, Gwen Kerfoot, Irene Wareham, Ethel Jones, Elizabeth Davies (charge-hand), Mr Gordon Jones (manager), Mr Horace Waterhause (managing director), Mr David Brewer (cutter), Hilda Williams, Margaret Hopwood, Emelda Davies, May Pendleton, Blodwen Jones, M Hughes(?)

GOODS MADE IN HOLYWELL.

Real Welsh Flannel,

made properly in the Old Welsh manner.

Does not shrink, and becomes softer by repeated washings.

(See sample, which has been in wear for eight years.)

Many flannels called Welsh Flannels are made elsewhere from foreign wools, which have not the good properties of REAL WELSH WOOL.

Be careful to ask, therefore, for REAL Welsh, or for the HOLYWELL Guaranteed quality, branded "WYNSANTA."

EXHIBITED BY

BROWN & Co.,

Mercers, CHESTER.

Goods made in various Mills and Factories in

HOLYWELL,

EXHIBITED BY

BROWN & Co.,

Mercers,

 CHESTER,

CONSIST OF

Real Welsh Flannels.
Real Welsh Flannels, guaranteed quality, branded "Wynsanta."
All-Wool Shirtings.
Flannel Shirtings.
Tweeds.
Shirts, Drawers.
Underclothing, Skirts etc.

———

The nature of the trade prevents the Millowners from dealing direct with drapers or the public, but information will gladly be given as to the warehousemen who distribute these goods.

TRADE ADVERTISEMENTS, c. 1903

These trade cards, issued by Brown & Co. of Chester, were very probably given away to visitors to St. Winefride's Well and Holywell, advertising as they do goods produced by woollen mills in the Greenfield Valley. Observe the note on the left-hand card to 'See sample, which has been in wear for eight years'. William Brown of this company helped form the Welsh Flannel Manufacturing Co. in 1874, producing the merchandise listed above. Queen Victoria is reputed to have ordered her flannel underwear from the Holywell mills. The last one in the town closed in the 1980s.

GREENFIELD VALLEY, c.1910

Taken from the top of Bryn Celyn, this view of the lower end of the Valley and the Dee Estuary is dominated by the six-storey lower cotton mill building (renamed Victoria Mills when it became a flour mill in the 1850s) and the Flour Mill Pool. In the foreground is the Holywell to Greenfield road. The buildings shown include Mount Pleasant Cottages and New Quay and Old Quay Cottages.

GREENFIELD FROM STRAND WOODS HOLYWELL.

LILYWHITE LTD
THE PHOTO PRINTERS

WHITE HOUSES

A splendid view across the meadow mill pool in the Greenfield Valley towards the Plough Inn and farm to the right. To the left, high on the bank, stands a row of cottages known as White Houses. A sale document of 1919 described them as being a block of six brick-built and slated cottages, all having large and productive gardens. On 18 April of that year the *County Herald* reported: 'Lot 37 White Houses were sold to Mr Kerfoot Roberts for £250'. The internal layout of each cottage varied, with Nos 4 and 6 having only a kitchen, back kitchen, and one bedroom. Rents ranged from £3 18s 0d to £5 4s 0d yearly.

MOTOR OMNIBUS, 1905

July 1905 saw the introduction of a regular motor omnibus service between the town and Holywell Station at Greenfield. The single-decker bus pictured here was one of two vehicles used by the London & North Western Railway Company, the other being a double-decker, and both were painted in the company's colours of chocolate and white. The tyres were made of solid rubber, but travelling was reported to be smooth and comfortable along most of the road. The drivers dressed in everyday clothes, although the conductors wore blue serge uniforms and caps.

STEAM LORRY, 1905

In 1905 the London & North Western Railway Company brought into service their steam lorry. With a maximum speed of 5 miles per hour, it was part of the replacement of the horse-drawn omnibuses provided by hotels such as the Kings Head and Lambert's to ferry passengers and parcels to and from the station. A 1912 report said: 'The vehicular connection with the station at one time was an old white horse, a rickety four-wheeler, and a driver that Dickens would have revelled in portraying and working into one of his inimitable sketches of quaint characters'.

The Station, Holywell.

Scotcher's Series.

HOLYWELL STATION, 1905

Rail travel arrived in Greenfield in May 1848 with the opening of Holywell Station on the London & North Western Railway Company's Chester to Holyhead line. The station expanded throughout the 19th century, an extra two platforms and a subway being added. Looking towards Mostyn, we see to the left the main buildings, designed by Francis Thompson, and Platform 1, with the slow and fast down lines. A brick building (centre) served Platforms 2 & 3, while on the far right is Platform 4's timber-built waiting-room. The station changed its name to Holywell Junction on 1 July 1912, when theHolywell branch line and the new Holywell Town station opened.

HOLYWELL BRANCH LINE, 1912

It is 1 July 1912, and the Holywell branch line has just been opened. The new station sign 'Holywell Junction' has replaced the former 'Holywell Station', and excited passengers prepare to board the train for its inaugural trip to the new Town Station. Among them, standing close to the edge of the recently completed and gaily decorated bay platform, and wearing a large white bonnet, can be seen Miss Amy Scotcher.

97409 HOLYWELL FROM STRAND WOODS

THE LITTLE TRAIN, 1928

This card, posted on 27 August 1928, shows the 'Little Train' — as it was known locally — passing the
Flour Mill Pool on its return journey to Holywell Junction station at Greenfield. On the far bank of the pool,
from left to right, can be seen the terraced houses of Old Quay, Mount Pleasant, and New Quay.

ABBEY PAPER MILLS, c.1930

Owned by Grosvenor, Chater & Company Ltd, the Mills are pictured here in the late 1920s. During their long history they survived two near disasters, the first a serious fire in 1894. The second — and far more damaging — was the drying-up of St Winefride's Well in 1917, depriving the mills of the thousands of gallons of water they needed daily. Although water was eventually restored to the well, the flow was much reduced and unreliable, thus curtailing for some years the company's plans for expansion. After more than two centuries of manufacturing high quality paper and associated products, production ceased in the early 1980s. Much of Abbey Mills has since been demolished and replaced by modern office buildings.

TAI COED, c.1930

Tai Coed (Wood Houses) were built in the late 18th century to house the workers employed in Thomas Williams's copper works. This excellent view of the cottages, taken several years before their demolition, shows the wooden rain barrels outside each front door. On 14 October 1915, the *Flintshire Observer* reported a double tragedy at No 7. Sarah Catherine Jones, aged 30, had been found dead on her bed, and her husband, John Arthur, was huddled against the bedroom wall with severe throat wounds, dying soon afterwards. There was a lengthy inquest, and the jury returned a verdict of double suicide, it being said that Sarah had poisoned herself and John had died of self-administered wounds.

HAYDEN NUTTALL, c.1930

Tai Coed's best-remembered resident and local character, Hayden Nuttall settled there after spending many years as a merchant seaman, and found new employment underground as a pumpman at Englefield Colliery. Two of his peculiarities were that he coal-tarred most of the interior of his cottage and preferred to sleep in a hammock in the living-room. This photograph, one of only two known to exist of Hayden, was taken in Greenfield and shows him with his beloved clay pipe, without which he was rarely to be seen. His sailor's prowess with a needle and thread can be gauged by the stitches in his trousers.

Basingwerk Abbey, Holywell

BASINGWERK ABBEY, c.1915

The Abbey was founded in the 12th century, and flourished until its closure in 1536, eventually owning land in Cheshire and Derbyshire in addition to 1,500 acres in Flintshire. It was dismantled over many decades by industrialists building factories in the Greenfield Valley. The stonework remaining to be shown on this postcard was once part of the Abbey's church, monks' dormitory, and novices' quarters.

BASINGWERK ABBEY, c 1924

During the 1920s Basingwerk Abbey came into state ownership, and the remaining sections were preserved. To the left, scaffolding can be seen round the Abbey's warming-house, in which was one of the community's only two fireplaces, the other being in the kitchen. The central section held the monks' dormitory, while on the right are the remains of the chapter house. Here were held the daily meetings where the monks received instructions on their work. Here, too, breaches of the Abbey's rules were dealt with. Punishments varied from fasting on bread and water or eating alone, to, for more serious offences, solitary confinement, whipping, or even expulsion.

GREENFIELD NEAR HOLYWELL. "The Unique Series".

BASINGWERK ROW, 1905

This picture looks along Greenfield Road towards Holywell, with Basingwerk Row to the right and Paper Mill Row on the left. Basingwerk Row was described in 1895 as a block of thirteen houses including the post office and a shop with an off-licence (seen above), whose two parts were divided by a curtain. Known today as Basingwerk Terrace, the Row has been partly demolished. Paper Mill Row was levelled in the 1920s. In 1919 John Davies, who was running the shop, applied for the renewal of his licence, but was successfully opposed on the grounds that the combination of trades 'might encourage drinking among women customers and so lead to ruination in the home'.

GREENFIELD, c.1880

One of the earliest known photographs of the village, this view, looking from Basingwerk Abbey towards the coast, shows the recently-completed road bridge (centre) leading to Greenfield Wharf and spanning the Chester to Holyhead railway. The central part of Railway Terrace had to be demolished to make way for the new road and bridge, leaving the surviving white cottages on either side of the road. On the extreme right is Abbey Terrace. To the far left is Station Road and the Old Queen's Head building. The quiet country road in the foreground is the A548 coast road.

MOSTYN ROAD, 1909

Postmarked 13 December 1909, this picture of Mostyn Road, Greenfield, looking towards Mostyn, shows a tranquil coast road that is a far cry from the heavy traffic conditions along this stretch today. On the far right is Robert Foulkes's grocer's shop with a few of the locals sitting outside taking a break. The large white building next door was the local bank, while the building furthest away is the Packet House Hotel. Directly opposite Foulkes's shop stood the Crown and Anchor Inn.

MOSTYN ROAD, c.1904

This view, looking towards Station Road, is one of a set of six pictures of Greenfield taken by a Rhyl photographer, Rae Pickard. It shows in the left foreground the Packet House Hotel, with the Old Bank next door. Beyond that is Robert Foulkes's grocer's shop and the Liverpool Arms. Facing us on the extreme right is R H Jones's barber's shop in Station Road.

STATION ROAD, GREENFIELD

Seen here around 1910, this was for more than a century Greenfield's main street. The Royal Hotel, on the extreme right, was once the premier hotel and posting house in the village. Directly opposite is the Liverpool Arms, which closed in 1909; it was said to have had a large circular bar and a 'machine for the use of customers'. A precursor of today's one-armed bandits, this was an imitation gun, and customers scoring a hit had their penny returned. Rather lonely among several public houses, Ebenezer Chapel is just visible in the distance on the left of the road.

MISS CARRINGTON'S SHOP, c.1922

Before the arrival of supermarkets and superstores the village corner shop provided the essentials needed by the poorer classes. Miss Carrington, pictured here in Station Road, sold a wide variety of goods, ranging from cream cakes to sewing materials, and tea to picture postcards. Many of the goods on sale were not ready-packed. Items such as biscuits, tea, coffee, and sugar were weighed from large tins and sacks, so allowing poor families to buy very small amounts costing a few pennies.

PACKET HOUSE HOTEL

'Phone: 36 Holywell

GREENFIELD, HOLYWELL

————

Large and Small Parties Catered for

Teas and Refreshments   Open on Sundays

Accommodation for Visitors   Buses Pass Door

————

Proprietor   -   -   -   E. E. DAVIES

THE PACKET HOUSE HOTEL, c.1930

This postcard would have been used to advertise the hotel. During the 1920s and 30s the Packet House was a favourite stopping-point for coach parties travelling to and from Prestatyn and Rhyl. In 1904 there were eleven fully licensed public houses and hotels in Greenfield, in addition to eight beershops. The Packet, as it was then known, was among the most popular, having the added bonus of good stabling, although the Holywell licensing magistrates ordered Lord Hanmer, its owner, to spend £200 on maintenance as a condition for the renewal of his licence.

Greenfield Council School, Holywell.

Scotcher's Series.

GREENFIELD SCHOOL, 1910

Greenfield County Primary School first opened its doors on 5 September 1910. In 1912 a visiting inspector described the School as 'handsome and commodious'. His report continued: 'As standards I and II have to be taught for most subjects in close proximity in one classroom, it is recommended that far less talking should be allowed among the pupils than at present. The theoretical lessons on Home Management are very well conceived and a little demonstration is attempted at times. '

Detraining Horses at Holywell.

Scotcher, Holywell.5034.

DETRAINING HORSES AT HOLYWELL, 1909

August 1909, and officers and men of the Lancashire Territorials prepare to detrain at Holywell Station. They were on their way to a military camp at Caerwys (See pp71 and 72). Some 122 officers, 3,603 men, 90 horses, and 20 guns and wagons disembarked at Greenfield. The station area was crowded with onlookers wanting to be part of this unique event in the village's history.

LANCASHIRE TERRITORIALS, 1909

The carnival atmosphere of the day continued as the Territorials marched down Station Road en route to Caerwys, led by the regimental band and cheered on by the residents of Greenfield. The troops are here seen leaving Station Road, passing the Royal Hotel, Liverpool Arms, and the Crown and Anchor Hotel.

GREENFIELD CARNIVAL, 1949

Carnivals at Greenfield have always been eagerly anticipated, and that of 1949 was no exception. Together with the usual floats and stalls there was a special event — a football match between the young men and women of the village. Above is the women's team 'Greenfield United', the eventual winners of the match (aided by a sympathetic referee). Left to right: *Back row*: Vera Williams, Mona Barlow, Rita Jones, Margaret Roberts, Lil Roden, Jean Mackie, Barbara Jones, Brenda Carr. *Front row*: Amy England, Alice Tapley, May Jones, Maris Jones

THE BOOT, BAGILLT, 1916

Raphael Tuck & Sons published this 'Aquagraph' postcard for the *Flintshire Observer* around 1916. The road to the left led up the Boot Hill towards Holywell, and the Bagillt-Greenfield road is just visible to the right. From here on Tuesday, 22 June 1897 local residents began their celebrations to mark Queen Victoria's Diamond Jubilee, starting with a procession along a decorated route from the Boot to the Blossoms. 80 poor persons not receiving poor relief were given food parcels to the value of two shillings each, and festivities continued throughout the day, ending with a large bonfire in the evening.

PENTRE BACH, BAGILLT, 1916

This postcard was sent to Mr & Mrs Bithell of Sale, near Manchester, on 2 June 1916. The sender wrote: 'This view is the main road; here there is a pump in the footpath. They have no other water here, only rainwater, and we are having a drop now, the first since I came.' He has marked the pump with a cross, directly opposite the old Bethania Chapel.

BAGILLT HIGH STREET, 1923

'The Pentre', as this part of the High Street was known, was regarded as the centre of Bagillt, housing many of the village's businesses and traders. Pictured on the right, next to the Baptist Chapel, is one of the best-remembered, Will Hughes's barber's shop. This postcard was discovered in London in 1985 by the author. Posted in Bagillt on 24 August 1923, it had reached Ohio, USA, on the 27th via New York.

BLOSSOMS BAGILLT.

BLOSSOMS, 1915

Looking back down Bagillt High Street from the Blossoms in 1915, a time when most of the village's young men would have been away fighting in the 1914-18 war. To the left are Talbot Terrace and Boatman's Row, and just visible in the distance is the Corn Mill.

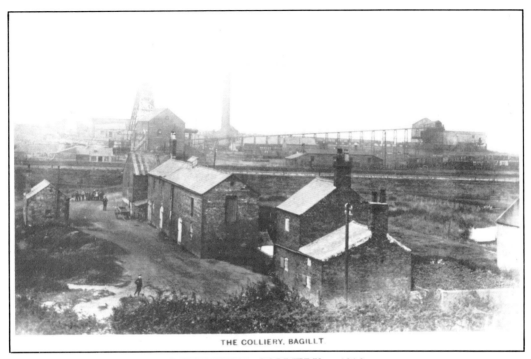

THE COLLIERY, BAGILLT.

BETTISFIELD COLLIERY, c.1923

One of the finest postcards depicting the local coalmining industry, this shows the gear head of the two main shafts, the engine house, the coal washing unit or screens, and various out-buildings. Mining was a major business in the area, and as other industries fell into decline in Bagillt, Bettisfield became a leading employer in the village. In 1891 boys and men worked the same hours, ranging from 54 to 74 hours a week.

Overall wages varied from 4s 9d to 25s 10d per week, depending on age and duties.

BAGILLT FROM STATION BRIDGE

LILYWHITE LTD
TRIANGLE HALIFAX

BAGILLT FROM STATION BRIDGE, c.1920

Bagillt had to wait until 1849 for a passenger station on the Chester to Holyhead line. Although the station provided a much-needed service, not all travel writers were impressed. An LMS route book detailing the track of the Irish Mail published in 1947 observed: 'Bagillt Station serves a village of unmitigated squalor, the chief eyesore on the Dee'. This view looks towards Greenfield, with the village to the left rising away towards Halkyn Mountain.

STATION ROAD, BAGILLT

Down this road commuters, day trippers, and visitors made their way to and from the station. The building closest to the level crossing gate was the crossing keeper's lodge, described in plans dated 1905 as a police house. On the opposite side of the road and partially hidden by a World War II air raid shelter is the Dee Inn. Bagillt station finally closed in 1966 after 117 years of service.

PARROT SCHOOL. "THE GADLYS." BAGILLT. NORTH WALES.

PARROT SCHOOL, 1911

This splendid postcard shows one of the most unusual businesses in Flintshire at the turn of the century: a school where parrots were taught to talk and sing. Postmarked 19 July 1911, it was sent to Mr N G Lambert of Sheffield, the message reading: 'Dear Sir, Just a line to say that I received your letter. I shall endeavour to get you the African Grey Parrot you require by the weekend. Yours faithfully, Mrs E Wright.' The lady pictured is probably Mrs Wright.

BAGILLT PAWN SHOP

Robert Williams's pawn shop was for many years in the old Forresters Hall in the centre of Bagillt. Poor families could stretch their income by 'pledging' items of clothing, jewellery, or furniture for a few shillings and then redeeming them the following week. In 1890 a man's suit fetched 2/- (10p) when pledged and cost an extra 3d (1½p) to get it back. Unredeemed items were auctioned after twelve months, an event eagerly awaited for the many bargains on offer.

CAERWYS HIGH STREET, 1908

This real photographic postcard, crisp in every detail, looks down towards the Cross and Water Street. The old Post Office can be seen on the left midway down the street. Among the various businesses in High Street in 1886 were two grocers, a baker, a provision and coal dealer, and the Cross Foxes public house. In 1895 the Postmaster of the 'Post, Money Order and Telegraph and Savings Bank' was John William Hughes.

THE CROSS AND HIGH STREET, c.1905

A slightly earlier view of High Street than that on the previous page, this time looking up from the Caerwys Cross. In March 1968 the Cross was moved to Mostyn Square, and a new tree was planted by the Earl of Plymouth to commemorate the 1968 Eisteddfod held at Caerwys.

MOSTYN SQUARE, CAERWYS.

"The Unique Series."

MOSTYN SQUARE

Mostyn Square and the present site of the Caerwys Cross at the turn of the century. A part of the Cross is just visible on the left, with Hereford House in the background. Another prominent feature of the Square was the Old Cross Keys Hotel seen here on the corner of the Square and Water Street.

70

Caerwys Camp. 1909.

Scotcher.Holywell. 4092

CAERWYS CAMP, 1909

'THE WAR IN CAERWYS! THE IMPENDING INVASION' 'A MEMORABLE ENCAMPMENT OF TERRITORIALS' These were some of the headlines the *Flintshire Observer* used to describe the camp at Caerwys during the summer of 1909. From headquarters situated at Bryngwyn Hall, Major General E C Bethune commanded some 385 officers, 11,763 men, 490 horses, and 136 guns and wagons spread throughout Caerwys and Afonwen. The Urban District Council claimed £87 7s 0d (later reduced) from the West Lancashire Territorial Association for damage caused to one of the roads by manoeuvres.

D.H.I.Y Camp at Caerwys, May 1910

CAERWYS CAMP, 1910

In May 1910 the Denbighshire Hussars Imperial Yeomanry and the Birkenhead company of the Army Service Corps set up camp on the low-lying ground near Afonwen, although much smaller than that of 1909. One of the main exercises was a route march taking in Caerwys, Mold, Wrexham, Llangollen, Corwen, and Ruthin. Sunday morning reveille sounded at 5.00am, and by 5.30am the troops were engaged in grooming horses and cleaning saddles. A church parade later was conducted by the Bishop of St Asaph.

W. 1561.   WHITFORD, NEAR HOLYWELL.

WHITFORD VILLAGE

During the 1860s and 1870s Whitford was described as an extensive parish in Holywell Union containing the townships of Tre-Mostyn, Tre-Llan, Bychton, Mertyn-Isglan, Mertyn-Uwchglan, Whitford-garn, Tre-Edenowen, and Tre-Abbot. Its 1871 population was 3,888. *Slater's Trade Directory* of 1883 remarked on the high standard of schooling and the parish's three noble seats. The community still thrives. Prominent in this early 1940s view are the Mostyn Arms, since renamed The Huntsman's, and the church.

RHEWL, c.1910

The prominent building on the right was the Feathers Inn (later the post office). Other public houses and hotels known to have been in Mostyn in the past include the White Lion, Red Lion, Swan, Cross Keys, Mostyn Arms Hotel, Lletty Hotel (known locally as the Honest Man), Glan y Don, King's Head, and Taliesin.

74

Mount Terrace, Rhewl, Mostyn.

RHEWL, c.1905

This view of a traffic-free Rhewl is deceiving, for shops were plentiful and varied in this part of Mostyn and would have been busy well into the evening. Although many Mostyn businesses registered themselves in trade directories (19th century yellow pages), Rhewl does not seem to have appeared until 1850, when it was spelled 'Rhwl'. As always, there was the inevitable public house. The building in the foreground was the Cross Keys Inn, for which the annual rental in 1928 was £16.

HALENDY, 1906

Halendy was once a thriving community, with a row of terraced houses, shops, and a chapel. In 1835 there was even a Mostyn public house called Halendy. The village has now completely disappeared, its buildings having been replaced by road improvements. This card was sent to Newcastle-on-Tyne on 23 May 1906. The sender, WH, who was staying at Mount Terrace, Rhewl, wrote: 'Can't get a decent card here. Am going to Rhyl tomorrow. Will send one from there'.

THE SQUARES, 1905

Known as the Squares, these three blocks of cottages on the coast road were built to house local miners and their families, those in each block sharing a communal bakehouse and other basic utilities. Although they appeared identical, their interior layout differed. The fire provided heating, hot water, and a place to cook meals. And, since collieries did not yet provide bathing facilities, miners had to wash in a tin bath at their own firesides.

TREVOR HOUSES

On the Mostyn road between Greenfield and Llannerch y Môr, Trevor Houses (Tai Trevor) were two parallel rows of cottages, forty-six in all, and a shop. Like similar cottages, they were originally occupied by mining families working at nearby collieries. The two rows were known as 'Heaven and Hell', this 1950s photograph showing 'Hell'. Sadly, Trevor Houses fell foul of the housing policies of the 1960s and were demolished.

MOSTYN STATION, 1905

Mostyn station opened on 1 May 1848. The building, like that at Holywell, was designed by Francis Thompson. Although Mostyn was no more than a village, passenger facilities were excellent compared with those of similarly-sized stations. This view looks west towards Ffynnongroyw. The iron works sidings and Mostyn Quay are on the right. In the left foreground is the goods shed, with the station buildings just behind. In 1905 the station had four platforms, reached by the covered footbridge seen in the distance.

Mostyn Quay   Holywell

MOSTYN QUAY, 1905

This rare postcard shows in the foreground a Mersey Flat, a small cargo vessel. Passenger steamers sailed regularly from the quay to the Wirral and Liverpool. By the mid 20th century Mostyn Quay could berth ships up to 2,500 tons displacement and 275 feet long. The longest of the three quays is 510 feet, served by road and rail, and had electric and steam cranes. Typical cargoes were cement, esparto grass (for the Greenfield paper mill), timber, pulp, china clay, and ore. In 1874 a return trip from Mostyn to Liverpool on the sailing steamer *Swiftsure* cost 2s 6d for a fore cabin and 3s 6d for one aft.

MOSTYN QUAY.

MOSTYN QUAY, c.1908

This view looks inland, and again 'flats' are moored at the quayside. That on the right, the *Temple*, was powered by both sail and steam and has a funnel, unlike its companion. Directly opposite Mostyn Quay was the Mostyn Arms Hotel, a favourite with sailors and dock workers. Here passengers could hire a horse and carriage to continue their journey. *Slater's Trade Directory* of 1856 lists the Post Office as being at Mostyn Quay, letters arriving by 'foot post' from Holywell; the postmistress then was Elizabeth Jones.

MOSTYN IRON WORKS, 1908

Incorporated on 13 April 1887, the Darwen & Mostyn Iron Co. Ltd took over from the Mostyn Iron & Coal Co. Ltd the running of the huge iron works alongside the dock. The factory employed many local people, and its enormous furnaces dominated the skyline of the village. Today very little shows where the now demolished works once stood.

MOSTYN HALL FIRE BRIGADE, c.1910

Many events and festivals were held in the grounds of Mostyn Hall, and Mostyn Hall Fire Brigade usually gave a demonstration of its skills, including life saving and 'pompier' ladder drills. Other brigades took part, and competitions were organised between them. Country house owners often formed their own brigades of uniformed firemen, usually from men employed on the estate. This steam fire engine would have been used to protect Mostyn Hall and its outbuildings, and probably also to attend fires in the village.

MOSTYN, c.1922

Leaving Mostyn, we look back towards the village, with the chimneys of the iron works emitting plumes of smoke into the sky. On the right, partly hidden by trees, is the Mostyn Arms Hotel. Mostyn station, with its variety of buildings, occupied the land to the left.

East End of Ffynnon Groew.

FFYNNONGROYW

This view, showing the approach to Ffynnongroyw from Mostyn, and taken from the east end of the mining village, was produced as a postcard around 1904-5. The road to the left led to Garth Mill, Llinegr Hill, and Pen y Ffordd.

FFYNNONGROYW, 1906

Slater's *North Wales Trade Directory* of 1868 listed the following businesses in the village, although probably others were not included. Grocers and dealers in sundries: William Davies; Robert Ellis; John Evans; and Hugh Williams. Linen and woollen drapers: John Hughes. The post mistress then was Eliza Hentage. Slater's *Directory of Flintshire* commented: 'Letters from all parts arrive (from Holywell) at half past nine morning and are despatched at twelve minutes past five evening . . . Mostyn Quay is the nearest money order office.' By 1889 the Railway Tavern and Farmer's Tavern had joined the Crown shown in the 1868 edition of *Sutton's Trade Directory*.

POINT OF AYR COLLIERY, 1907

Following the first boreholes in 1865, the colliery was well established by the 1890s, producing good quality coal, and employing 75 ponies underground. As in many other mining communities, most local people relied either directly or indirectly on the pit for their living. This postcard shows the gearheads of No 1 and No 2 main shafts and, to the right, the old wooden jetty where ships such as the *Talacre* would load with coal for Ireland and elsewhere. In 1922 half of Point of Ayr's output was being sent to Ireland.

POINT OF AYR LIGHTHOUSE

POINT OF AYR LIGHTHOUSE

Entering service at Talacre in September 1777, the lighthouse cost £353 18s 4d. Initial difficulties included the lamps smoking and clouding the lights and the oil freezing in winter, but a far bigger problem was the claim that the lighthouse could be seen further away by day than the light at night. In 1883 it was replaced by a small lightship in the Dee estuary, and just over two hundred years after being built, it was offered for sale as a five-floored detached residence: 'one of the more out-of-the-ordinary properties and a snip at £15.000'.